The World of
Teens part 1

Shaykh Muhammad Yahya Ibn Faruq

Third Edition

IT'S JUST A BIT OF HARMLESS FUN...

THE POWER OF DUA

TEENAGE ROMANCE

DHIKR DHIKR

SMOKING DRUGS

WHAT'S WRONG WITH DATING?

IT'S ONLY A SPLIFF...

 An Nasihah Publications

First Edition 2004
Second Edition 2008
Third Edition 2011

An Nasihah Publications
P O BOX 7737
LEICESTER LE5 5XU. United Kingdom

Email : theworldof_teens@yahoo.com

©An Nasihah Publications

British Library Catalogue-in-Publication Data.

A CIP record for this book is available from the British Library.

ISBN 978-0-9548727-0-3

Distributors in the UK: Azhar Academy, London
www.azharacademy.com

Printed in Turkey by Imak Ofset Printers : isa@imakofset.com.tr

Design & Artwork by Rizwan Ahmed : riz160@yahoo.co.uk

Contents

Comments and Feedback

"Before reading this book i did'nt have a clue what the true meaning of life was, all that i had involved boys, money and friends. I never used to listen to anyone and just did things of my own will. Alhamdulillah after reading your book I realised the mistakes that I have made and a wish to repent grew within me. Jazakallh. For this book has personally helped me . (Muslim Sister. 15)

"... The World of Teens is great. Mashallah i really hope you continue with these books... (Muslim Sister. 13)

".....May Allah reward you for your efforts in writing this book. May Allah give me and other teenagers the strength to become good practising Muslims..." (Muslim Sister. 14)

"I read ur book and thoroughly enjoyed it. May Allah reward you for your loyal service to Deen." (Muslim Sister. 18)

"...The World of Teens, was easy to read, less time consuming and straight to the point. I enjoyed reading it from the minute i picked it up and finished it all in one go..." (Muslim Sister . 19)

"...A very blessed task, may Allah make it beneficial..."
(Shaykh Yusuf Motala . Founder of Darululoom Bury. Uk)

'Allah willing, this book will help teenagers change their lifestyle and come to the right path. May Allah, the Almighty accept Muhammad Yahya's effort and enable him to do more in future for the guidance of youth.'
(Shaykh Daud Falahi. Lecturer of Hadith at Darululoom Leicester uk.)

"In today's time, when the youth are so involved in major sins that it seems to have become an accepted part of life, there was a dire need for a book of this sort to be written. Alhamdu lillah, the author has addressed many important topics related to the younger generation in a brief but concise manner. The language and style used will be familiar to the youth. The humorous and light-hearted approach is sure to hold the readers interest throughout. If these major issues can be openly talked about and explained by parents and teachers at an early stage in life, there is hope Insha'Allah that bad habits will not take form. Instead these young people can develop into good, pious individuals who will be the leaders of tomorrow. May Allah accept the author's efforts and make it a means of his salvation in the hereafter. Ameen."
(Shaykh Yusuf Boodi. Senior Hifdh Teacher and former A-Level co-ordiantor.)

Acknowledgements

Special acknowledgements must go to: my respected parents and teachers who were always giving that extra word of encouragement to keep me going; my wife & son who were there to support me; my brothers and sisters for their continuous help despite my shortcomings; my English teacher Sir Siraj Lambat for his help once again; brother Abid Russell for the thorough editing and advice on many issues despite his busy schedule , Mufti Ebrahim Moosa for his assistance in setting the book; brother Rizwan Ahmed for the beautiful design and artwork; all those young teens out there who sent their vital suggestions and feedback which compelled me to continue; and all those who assisted with the publication of this book. May Allah grant them all and the whole Muslim Ummah a Hayatan Tayyibah (a happy peaceful life). Ameen.

Foreword

All Praise is due to Allah, the Lord of the worlds, and his blessings are on his noble Prophet Muhammad sallallahu alayhi wasallam, his Companions, noble wives and all those that follow him till the day of judgement.

It is a saying of our beloved Prophet Muhammad sallallahu alayhi wasallam that 'from amongst all the temptations (fitnah) that shall come upon my ummah after me, the fitnah of immorality and indecency shall be the most severe and the most detrimental to one's Iman.'

The age we live in today is an age wherein modesty has steeped to a low level that was unimaginable a few centuries ago. Yes, vices have existed throughout history, but they were understood and accepted as vices, never in history has immodesty and indecency reached to such a degree where it has been accepted and taken up as a whole new style of living!

The world of media- newspapers, TV, magazines etc- have dedicated a great part of themselves in service to this new world-wide fashion of nudity, indecency, and immorality, leading to everyone being tainted and affected by its wickedness and corruption.

Regrettably, this wave has forced itself into the lives of many Muslims.

Hence there was a great need of the teachings of Allah ta'ala and the Prophet Muhammad sallallahu alayhi wasallam regarding such evils to be brought in front of humanity for the purpose that it may protect themselves and regain their treasure. With this in mind, (Moulana) Hafiz Muhammad Yahya wished to present this book to his own age group, taking their health, wealth and Iman into consideration, for it is the youth that are the foundations of our world.

It is my du'a that this book becomes a means of guidance and benefit for every young and old, male and female of the Ummah. (Ameen)

(Sheikh) Ismail Ahmed Patel.
(Principal & Founder of Darul Uloom Leicester UK)

Introduction

In the Name of Allah, the Most Beneficent, the Most Merciful. All Praises be to Allah ta'ala and peace and Salutations be upon the Best of Mankind: Muhammad.

Alhamdulillah, by the grace of My Lord the third edition of part one is now in your hands. It is only Allah who has made these books a huge success, helping many teenagers change their lives and reform themselves into instrumental individuals. I pray to Allah that he accepts this in His court and grants us all sincerity. Ameen.

Looking around society today, we see many a youth who were once innocent and sprightly children who playfully ran around in the parks and playgrounds, or were held lovingly in the hands of their caring mothers. But sadly these same individuals have diverted and fallen into the trap of shaytan-a trap that waits in pursuit to lure innocent teenagers entering the years of adolescence. In a world where we see disobedience, disrespect and immorality becoming the norm, it seems very hard for young Muslim boys and girls to disconnect themselves from all the temptations and become a 'Junayd

Baghdadi' or a 'Rabi'ah Basriyyah. Yet we have learnt that amidst a nation of idol worshippers Allah ta'ala made a noble and pure messenger emerge, he stood all alone against the evil practices and, through the help of Allah, prevailed. With this in mind my main intention is to provide the young traveller a clearing and a path through the dense fog and the swampy mires that he/she encounters through the golden years of teenage life.

This book has been split into several parts to make it easy for the 'traveller' to digest and has been written in the language and style of teens. Insha'allah if every young person that comes across this book picks it up and reads it with an open mind and an intention to improve, then Allah ta'ala will surely guide the one who seeks the truth.

If you find any fault, then correct it I pray,
For no one is faultless except Allah
(Jalaaluddin Abd Ar Rahman As Sooyuti)

Muhammad Yahya Ibn Farouk
June 2011/ Rajab 1432.

Chapter 1

Challenging years

Dear Teenager

Your world is changing quicker now.
Your choices are unfolding.
The future lies within your grasp,
A vital force worth moulding.
Your task is not a simple one;
Your course has not been set.
You must avoid the obstacles,
Steer clear of every threat.
The pressures come from all over,
Examples good and bad.
Be special through the company you keep,
The friends who strengthen, add.
Don't ever loose control
And let the others steer your way.
Your life's a gift for you to shape,
With an invincible force.
Remember some are wise,
While there are some who are otherwise.
Aim high, make us proud.
You may seek all the answers:
Be content to find a few.
Don't grow impatient with the world–
Tomorrow's world is you...

(Adapted from 'Dear Teenager'
By B. Wilmer)

Every action in the world today has a beginning, middle & an end. The beginning is to get started on an errand; the end is the process of packing up, while the most crucial part is the middle, where the job gets done. Take the example of driving a car. The beginning is to start the engine and to manoeuvre onto the road; the end part is arriving at the destination in which the car slows down. But the main part of driving is between the two. Similarly is the case of life. Childhood is its beginning, old age its end and teenage life its middle and most crucial.

For this reason we see that a boy or a girl reaches his/her peak at this age, everything is in order, he has the strength of a grown man, intelligence increases so that he begins to fathom things around him, reasoning bursts out with a million 'Why's,' e.g. 'WHY am I here?' 'WHY do I have to do what they say?' Etc...

When something is at its crucial point in development, it needs all the attention and care possible. For example, when an apple tree is in its first years of bearing fruit, then the farmer's main concern is the protection of the apples. Using all sorts of pesticides to keep spiders, bacteria and fungus at bay, the farmer protects the fruits. Likewise teenagers are at such an important part of development that if they are left in the streets and clubs, (as we see today) then no doubt, they are open to 'bacteria,' which will crawl over them and infect them.

Now, in order to keep the apples growing perfectly, the farmer needs to make sure that large amounts of disinfectants are not used otherwise it will result in the fruit disintegrating due to the chemicals. Too little an amount will also cause them to rot. Again this example can be reflected onto the teenager that too many restrictions will cause him to become an unsociable person, while too less will make him undisciplined. So, the farmer needs such a chemical, which will make the apples grow in a way that they are accepted by world consumers. Once that chemical is found then the apples are protected and ready to be exported. Again reflecting this very example on a teenager a 'chemical' is needed that will aid the teen to the shore. the responsible powers of western culture began the quest for this 'super spray' to control the 'teen tree.' What did they come up with?

Intoxicants & women!

Keep them busy with drugs, alcohol and women. Then we can get on with our chores while they rot!

This 'chemical' was designed to control the teen, but as we witness today, it was totally unsuccessful. The only 'chemical', which is fit for this very delicate age, is ISLAM; the most moderate, natural and cool religion.

After the creation of mankind, Allah subhanahu wata'ala set his syllabus for each human. Each individual after completing the syllabus and passing his examinations, shall attain success through

Paradise.(Jannah) God forbid any student failing would face severe consequences through punishment in hellfire (Jahannam).

It has been stated in a Hadith reported in 'Bukhari & Muslim' (two famous authentic books in the field of the 'sayings & actions of the prophet sallallahu alayhi wasallam.')

'Abu Hurairah radhiyallahu anhu (may Allah be pleased with him) reports that the Prophet Sallallahu alayhi wasallam said: "Jahannam (hell) has been covered with temptations and Jannah (paradise) has been covered by difficulties."

Therefore a person who follows his desires in this temporary world shall fall into Jahannum and the one who controls his desires and bears the difficulties of not having all the unlawful fun shall enter the garden of eternal bliss and pleasure.

In the build up to exams, a candidate with more abilities is required to cover a more difficult syllabus. Likewise, in life, the candidate with the most abilities is a teenager and therefore the temptations are much severe, so the reward is much greater.

As stated in a Hadith:'Abu Hurairah radhiyallahu anhu (may Allah be pleased with him) reports that the Prophet Sallallahu alayhi wasallam said: "Seven (types of) people whom Allah will grant shade under his throne on that day when there shall be no shade except His;

1. A just ruler
2. A young man/woman who grew up in the worship of Allah.
3. A person whose heart is always attached to the masjid.
4. Two persons who's friendship is based only on the pleasure of Allah, they meet for Him and disperse for Him. (they have no ulterior motives for meeting)
5. A man who is called by a pretty and honourable girl (to sin) but he says ' I fear Allah' (and abstains).

6. A person who gives in charity discreetly to such an extent that his left hand is unaware of what his right hand gave.

7. A person who, sitting alone remembers Allah and tears begin to flow.

'Bukhari & Muslim)

Chapter 2

Teenage Romance

One of the first tests a teenager goes through on reaching the door step of puberty is that he/she begins to recognise the opposite sex through a different eye. Before it was just a 'girl or a boy'. But now it's a **beautiful girl** or a **handsome boy**.
This test is very hard in its initial stages, especially when they are sooo many about.

But not to worry, no test is set without having a solution. It's not so difficult once a grasp has been gained on how to tackle it. In this case we have a very cunning being who has taken the responsibility of tricking candidates. And who may this be? His name is well known to all: **'Shaytan'**
Yes, we have all heard of him and his army in all spheres: he pops up somehow, somewhere surreptitiously.

Ok, let's take a look at how he has managed to claw his way into this with his bag of tricks.

He has exploited this topic so much that it has become impossible to detect this as a real test. Wherever you look, it's either a man or a woman being displayed in the most indecent way, be it the billboards, newspapers or internet 'pop-ups', immorality has become so rampant that it makes us think it is natural and a norm.

But, NO! It is a test, remember!

To tackle this, firstly let's take at look at how the Qur'an has guided us for this: -

"Tell the believing men to lower their gaze and be modest. That is purer for them. Lo! Allah is Aware of what they do." (24:30)

Allah, in his infinite bounty has guided us through this. Well you may be wondering, "What about the girls? Huh, they're not any better!" Well read on, in the very next verse Allah Subhanahu Wata'ala states:

"And tell the believing women to lower their gaze and be modest... And turn unto Allah together, O believers, in order that you may succeed." (24:31)

The main cure for this is to lower the gaze. A point to remember is that the first accidental gaze is forgiven but the second gaze will be penalised accordingly or if the first gaze is prolonged to the extent that you start to drool all over your clothes. Obviously it's hard when they just come in front of you. Well try it, once, twice and soon you shall feel your head jerking away automatically. (Don't worry, you won't become a robot!)

The rewards for lowering the gaze are magnificent. Let's take a look at the Hadith of the Prophet, sallallahu alayhi wasallam:

Sayyidina Abu Umamah (may Allah ta'ala be pleased with him) said that the Prophet Sallallahu alayhi wasallam said:

"No Muslim gazes at a woman's beauty for the first

time and thereafter lowers his gaze except that Allah ta'ala creates within him the ability to perform worship of which the sweetness he himself can taste." (Reported by Imam Ahmad)

Remember exactly the same virtue exists for the girls! You might think "it's only a bit of harmless fun" or 'He or She looks so alluring, I just can't help myself.

'Her eyes are absolutely hypnotising...

The radiant smile...."

But you know, 'don't judge a book by its cover'

In the same way don't take this on face value she may seem very beautiful, but alas will she remain beautiful forever? Will the same skin remain forever? Think! If she suddenly comes up with boils! Will she still be sooo beautiful? Don't deceive yourself!

Once a person came to the Prophet Sallallahu alayhi wasallam and said 'O prophet of Allah! Give me permission to commit fornication.'

The prophet Sallallahu alayhi wasallam told him to come closer and asked him-to the nearest meaning- 'Would you like it if someone committed adultery with your mother or with your sister?"

The man exclaimed in horror "Of course not!" Similarly, the woman that you wish to commit adultery with is someone's sister or mother."

The prophet Sallallahu alayhi wasallam thereafter made du'a for him and he was protected. (Reported by Imam Ahmad)

Subhanallah! Look how the messenger of Allah Sallallahu alayhi wasallam explained to this young Sahabi. Think that the girl you are befriending is someone's sister or someone's daughter. Would you like if someone did that to your sister or daughter? If you do, then you need yourself checked out, ok! It's not natural!

Take as an example a toy car which is spring loaded,

when you push it back and then let go, it goes forward according to how much you wound it back. The case of the eye is the same, the more you use it to view unlawful things the more it will go ahead.

A look, then a smile, then a nod of the head, Then a talk, then a promise, then the warmth of the bed...

One thing leads to another.

The first step is viewing the girl or boy, the first glance. Once you start then Shaytan starts inflating the image like a balloon so then she or he looks so beautiful that 'there's just no one like her.'

But, as you may have already seen that these relationships don't last very long. Because when the accursed Shaytan observes that this is not going according to plan then he puts a pin in the balloon. And now she looks sooo ugly, just like when a balloon bursts what do you do? Dump it!

The important question to consider is this: imagine yourself as a married person and in years to come (Allah forbid), you realise that the girl you are with was once involved with someone else. How would you feel?

You want to have a pure and clean partner that hasn't done anything bad, similarly your partner deserves the same. What is better, a bird that is only yours and doesn't go round trying to attract others or the bird that, is ever ready to fly away? Yes, dear brothers and sisters that is the difference between relationships before marriage and a relationship through marriage. How pure and clean is Islam that it has acknowledged that a boy needs a girl in life and a girl needs a boy, therefore let your first kiss, your first touch be to that girl who is going to be the partner of your life.

Hopefully by now we should realise that to stop ourselves from something we should not go near it.

Now, what if we go to high school where the classrooms are mixed? And to avoid intermingling in that sense becomes impossible? Well, not to worry! Ibn Kathir has narrated that Once Sayyidina Umar (radhiyallahu anhu) asked a Sahabi what he knew taqwa be. The reply is an indirect answer to the above dilemma.'Have you ever walked along a thorny road where each side is covered with thorns?' The Sahabi asked.

"Yes" Umar Radhiyallahu Anhu replied.

"So then what did you do?" the Sahabi went on.

"I collected my clothes so as not to get pricked by the thorns."

"That is taqwa!" the Sahabi exclaimed.

It would be ideal if this generation and all that follow had the option of attending single sex schools where intermingling doesn't occur, but unfortunately at present there simply aren't enough of these schools to go round. But we can't just sit back and say, "O let this generation of youth rot and we will look after the generations to come". No! You are also humans and have a right to be looked after.

The journey is difficult- the traveller still has to travel, but it will have to be in a more careful way. Now, what does one mean by careful?

Make a good effort by talking to the opposite sex to the minimum: only talking when it is necessary. Let people call you what they want, let them say : 'He's backwards! Loner!'

How long will they carry on?

In the end they will tire. Wont they?

But tell me, if we do talk and are top in our friend's books and they begin to say:

'Yeh! Man this guys cool' and (Allah subhanahu wa ta ala forbid) we go to Jahannum, then how long will that be for?

Not for a year, not for two years. But for eternity. Is it really worth it?

Make du'a to Allah that 'O' Allah I am weak, please

help me!' and keep your gaze down. Insha'allah, Allah will make your years pass easily. Don't ever let Shaytan fool you: "Oh come ON man, how old are you? Where you gonna get this kinda fun again? Just look at those pretty eyes and that lovely smile."

Keep yourself busy in fruitful activities so you don't start dreaming away. Remember: "an idle mind is the devil's workshop." Dreaming is the worst because from dreaming you will get all your ideas. Don't sit alone doing nothing read good material. Increase your knowledge.

Think of ways by which you can help the weak and poor of the world. Organise activities for yourself and those friends who don't have any illicit relationships but DON'T let your imagination take you away! Shaytan is your enemy, he wants YOU to join him in going to Jahannum, say 'no' once! Twice! Then he'll leave you alone for the time being and will try to get you another way. Be vigilant!

Allah has stated in the Qur'an "And follow not the footsteps of the devil. Lo! He is an open enemy for you." (surah 2 ayah 168)

Don't let peer pressure get to you. "Everyone's got one. They all live happily, I mean why? Why do I have to be the odd one? I stick out man, like a sore thumb!"

You may appear to look a loner in the eyes of some but remember in the eyes of Allah you really are a hero, while the others will be zero. Be your own judge, don't be the tail of others- whatever they do I do! You've got a brain, haven't you? Was this why I was created? To enjoy girls only? No, no, give your brain a hard knock if it says yes! Your friends may all look happy but believe you me they die inside as soon as they see their so -called partner talking to another. Oh my, my, they can't say anything but they melt inside, their nights are spent sleeplessly in thinking "What can I do next to impress my bird?"

As for you, YOU can sleep peacefully, with no worries. 'Aaah...' what a peaceful life knowing that Allah loves you and so does everyone else. While those people know very well that they are in the disobedience of Allah and the Almighty Lord is displeased with them. Is that the life you want to live? An artificial life! Standing in front of the mirror for an hour just trying to get the 'mascara' sorted out or the hair into a nice bun so he looks at me or casting down shirt after shirt in case she doesn't like my choice of designer labels .

For Allah's sake: think! Live naturally how Allah has made you. I'm not saying don't have a bath. No, but I'm saying live naturally. Insha'allah if all these points are taken into consideration then you shall prosper and will remember your youth as a fruitful one, not a bitter, artificial one!

Allah ta'ala has given each of us the choice to choose between right and wrong and it is through exercising this power of choice shall we be rewarded or punished. Our nafs (ego) is like a snake that can never die and the more we listen to its demands the more stronger it becomes. You know today we think that oh man its just a bit of fun i mean come on I'm not gonna have sex with her just chilling, that is the trick of the devil one thing leads to another so stop yourself before its too late.

Ibn Kathir a famous commentator of the Quran has mentioned an amazing incident that once at the time of Bani Israeel (the nation of Musa Alayhis Salam) there were three brothers who had a beautiful sister. It so happened that due to unforseen circumstances they had to travel, in those days journeys were quite arduous and long so they could not take their sister. But who could they leave her with?

After a little contemplation they all agreed that the young Barsisa was the only man suitable, known for his piety and worship of Allah ta'ala. It took much persuasion to make Barsisa agree to have a little house built for her next to his monastery. The brothers left and Barsisa continued his daily chores but in addition to this, every day he would stop his worship, go out and place food outside the girls house, a few weeks passed and shaytan whispered to him, 'Come on she ain't no animal! How can you leave it outside at least knock on her door and place the dish inside!" Barsisa thought hey that's true. Nothing wrong with that and so began his destruction...

A few weeks later the devil whispered again; 'Look she's all alone at least ask her how she is, if she needs anything etc.' And Barsisa began asking if she required anything, before long these questions developed into long conversations. Shaytan then put a thought in his head: 'You're a well respected person, people pass by whilst you talk to this girl, of course you're just asking how she is, but what will others be thinking. It's safer for you to go inside and talk, don't look at her. Just enter and you can converse behind a door. As this new scenario began

Barsisa found himself spending half an hour on a regular basis getting to know this girl but he had still not laid his eyes on her.

After a few days Barsisa's desires overcame him and he removed the covering that lay between them, as his eyes fell on her, he went as far as committing the evil act of fornication. Realising what he had done, Barsisa ran away to his monastery.

Nine months later the girl herself came to the monastery carrying a baby and said to Barsisa:

"Look what you've done! You made me pregnant and now I have given birth!" He became worried for he knew if the brothers came and saw this he was a finished case so the once upon a time pious Barsisa conspired to Kill.

He thought that if he killed the girl what would he do with the baby and if he killed the baby then the girl would most certainly testify against him. In the end he resolved to kill both!

Allahu Akbar.

Coincidently the brothers arrived the very same week and asked the whereabouts of thier sister.

Barsisa let flow crocodile tears and said' alas she fell ill and breathed her last.' The brothers were greatly grieved by this news, but nevertheless thanked Barsisa for his service, paid their respects at the grave shown to them and went home. That night shaytan came in all their dreams and told them the truth.

Barsia was exposed, the brothers came and dug the place they were shown in the dream and to thier utter disbelief found their sister with a baby!

Immediately Barsisa was taken to court and a verdict was issued that he should be put to the gallows. As he stood there with his head in the gallows shaytan appeared before him and said do you know who i am? It was I who gave the brothers the idea to leave their sister with you. It was I who told you to do all those things and only I can take you form this mess and put you back to where you were. All you have to do is bow your head down to me and ill sort everything out . The helpless Barsisa did so and the gallow came and he was no more...

Dear girls and boys out there, think! this is our enemy from the highest ranks of piety to the lowest ranks of fornication, murder and shirk (disbelief in Allah tala). Let us take heed from this incident for intelligent is he who reflects on the blunders of others. Remember drops make oceans, pebbles make mountains. (and pennies make pounds).

Once you begin a relationship or any sin your ego will crave for another and something bigger and in the end there's nothing but sadness and misery , why? Because in haram there can never be real happiness its just temporary check the following article out from the Daily Mail;

"As Claire lay in bed shaking, crying and sweating, unable to contemplate moving from under her duvet, she knew something was terribly wrong. A dreadful fever? No. In fact, Clare's symptoms were the result of her clinical addiction to love. Incredible though it may sound, experts agree that love addiction is a medical condition which can cause as much as physical and emotional affliction as being hooked on drugs or alcohol.'Everytime a relationship ended, it felt as though my life had disappeared,' recalls Clare, 46, a radio and TV broadcaster (46! Read on and find when all this started thats why the poet say Watch your thoughts before they become your words, your words before they become actions, your actions before they become your habits, your habits before they become your characters and your characters before they became your destiny..). But it was much more than just the proverbial broken heart. 'Some of the relationships had lasted barely a few dates, but I'd find myself unable to work or sleep and would end up entertaining suicidal thoughts. ' I was like a naive teenager in a womens body obsessing about men and my own desire, to be the perfect girlfriend, believing that this would make men love me . I was addicted to the initial high you get in those first few weeks and months of a relationship. That was my drug, my euphoria. The first signs of my addictive personality emerged when I was 14...

I had huge crushes on boys and would always brood over them. I developed an obsession with my weight and the scales would dictate what kind of day I would have. If I was a pound lighter then the day before, I'd be happy. But if I weighed more I'd be in the depths of despair. When I had a boyfriend it would dominate my life to such an extent that I'd spend hours in my room trying on ten different outfits.

A few years into my marriage the old habits crept back in. I left my husband to experiment with other men I moved out of our home into a rented flat, got a job on channel 4 news and pored over magazine articles telling me what I should do now that I was single. Top of the list was meeting new people, so I decided to run the London Marathon and met my first post (after) marriage boyfriend while we were running. Dan and I dated for a year and the relationship was quickly intense sexually and emotionally because that's what I craved.' It marked the start of a decade of unhealthy, addictive relationships with men. I finished with Dan after that exciting initial period ended because I craved intensity again. Until I locked eyes with Jake in a bar one night and felt as though I'd been hit by a rock the feelings were so strong. He was married with a child, but we still had an affair that was to last eight years. During the Jake years I also met a guy on a self- help conference who had a partner himself but this did not stop us enjoying ourselves. Then there was a man ten years my junior whom I met at an ITN news party and he made it clear to me that he wanted me. In the end I found myself on the kitchen floor contemplating an overdose because I was so bereft and lonely I felt I might die... **(Daily Mail Tuesday, April29, 2008)**

Well what can we say she was a definite player.. That's the true fact its never ending you doing it now you'll do it after your married and satisfaction will never come. May Allah make us understand.

Ok.
That was to do with the people who have not yet moved on to this path of getting a girlfriend/boyfriend, but who were maybe considering it.

Now let's discuss those candidates who have a GF/BF (G...) but inshallah want to change their lives cause they acknowledge that they have been in the net of Shaytan for a time.

My dear friends, although we transgress Allah's

commands, He never leaves us or forgets us. Allah says:

'(O Muhammad), tell My slaves who have oppressed themselves: Despair not of the mercy of Allah, for Allah indeed shall forgive all sins. Lo! He is the Forgiving, the Merciful. "(Surah39 ayaah53)

Repent to Allah! Yes, shaytan will probably put a last blow in, now, knowing that you will be leaving him.

"Are you in your senses? Allah to forgive YOU? After all those dates? All those kisses?

All that evil? Na bob, just leave it, you can't be forgiven! Might as well enjoy yourself, now that you're doomed."

Well tell him a Hadith as your goodbye words:

Narrated Anas (radhiyallahu anhu): Allah's messenger sallallahu alayhi wasallam said, "Allah the exalted has said: 'O son of Adam, I shall go on forgiving you so long as you pray to Me and hope for My forgiveness,

whatever may be your faults. O son of Adam, I do not care even if your sins should pile up to the sky; and should you beg pardon of Me, I would forgive you. O son of Adam, if you come to me with an earth full of sins and meet Me, not associating anything with Me (in worship), I would come to you with an earth full of forgiveness.'"
(At- Tirmidhi)

Blanked him straight! Alhamdulillah.

There are three conditions for the acceptance of repentance:
Have regret for doing the sin.
Have a firm intention never to do it again.
And leave that sin immediately.
So how DO you leave it? Again, Shaytan will come with another deception
"O man! How can you do that to her? All the years together, all those happy moments, no man we can't, I mean don't you even have a 'kind cell' in your body?"

Well tell him how can I **not** do it: all the days I slept with the anger of my Lord who fed me, clothed me, loved me, gave me parents, gave me a body, gave me a brain, the list is endless. Who is more worthy?

So, do it my friends, you don't have to say 'get lost', you can do it properly. I don't mean have one more date or anything. You've got a brain, work it out! Tell her in your own terms.

If you can't face her then write a note and leave it for her.

That "my dear beloved... joking, don't write that, write her normal name. Tell her that I really can't carry on I am sorry bye...

Finished! To the point.

No ifs or buts. If she's clever she'll understand, if not, then in due time she will. Or try helping her "I realized what I have been created for. My purpose of existence is not fun or blind enjoyment. For this reason I have decided to abandon those things which displease my Lord. Wassalam." Beautiful!

Flabbergasting! Imagine how happy Allah will be that My servant, despite of possessing the means to sin, declines only for Me. Allahu Akbar.

Remember if Allah wants to change someone either towards good or bad it does not take long. Fathom the fact that Allah likes you, that's why he gave you a chance to repent. Think of how many others there are that are still trapped. Make du'a for them. Allah decided that he wants to accept you, chose you from the rest. Now see the peace of life you shall experience. Feel the coolness of your eyes in salah. Your life will take an 180° turn towards good. Mashallah .And, again, don't be scared of what people will say. There will always be some people whom you will never be able to please, so just live for Allah, not for people.

Once there was a father and son walking through a town and with them they had a donkey. So on seeing this, the townsfolk exclaimed: "Look at these foolish

people! They have a donkey yet they do not ride it."
So the son mounted the donkey whilst the father
walked by his side. Upon passing another town the
townsmen said;

"How disrespectful is the son, he mounts whilst his
father strolls along."

So the son dismounted to make way for the father.
Those standing on the street corners of the next
town said,

"What an oppressor the father is, he mounts whilst
his son walks!" Hearing this, the father and son both
sat astride the beast and do you know what the
inhabitants of the next village said? They said "Do
these people have no consideration for the donkey?
They are burdening him with the weight of two! So
the father and son had only one last option, which
was to carry the donkey! The villagers jeered at
them and said, "how foolish! They have a conveyance
yet they become its conveyance." In the end, the
father and son became so frustrated that they

threw the donkey into the well. So you see people will never be happy with what you do. The best thing to do is to leave them to their own grumblings. And, finally, remember, that success comes in 'cans' and not 'cants.'

YOU CAN DO IT!!!

Chapter
3

Smoking

Yes, you thought teen life was just about girls, ha! You got it wrong mate! Public enemy number one 'Shaytan' doesn't give up so easily, he's got many in store for you, but don't worry we can do it together! Inshallah.

Ok let's get cracking on this case. We know the criminal.

We have to understand the effects of this treacherous plan, what it consists of and what it can do to us. Then we have to look for a cure, a proper preventive cure.

Let's take it one at a time,

Ok, Smoking!

'I wanna look cool!'

'I wanna look tough!'

'I don't wanna to be left out'

These are the usual reasons teens give for justifying the act that they do. True? Well, once again you live for people? Huh! Why? Are they so close to you? Do they shower you with presents just because you follow them?

They are fools themselves for opting for such a way of destruction and you're making a fool out of yourself by following them. Think!

Do you really wanna follow people blindly?

When people start up a business they do it

through careful strategic planning. So how can you choose a pattern of your life merely by looking at people!

So? What are you gonna think about? Is it going to be 'Benson & Hedges'? Or, 'Silk Cut'? Maybe even a cigar: more tobacco! Quicker we die!

Yes you may not think of that aspect when puffing away but it's a proven fact that smoking is a slow suicidal act.

And suicide is Haram (forbidden)

Allah says in the Holy Qur'an

"And do not Kill yourself (Nisa 29)

Come on! We don't need so many statistical facts; the consequences are visible with our own eyes. How many smokers have clean teeth? None! (Unless of course bleach is used as toothpaste.)How many smokers suffer from serious skin problems?

In the annual conference of the American Doctors Council which took place in Chicago in 1996, many doctors were amazed to note that the least harm smoking causes is that it arouses anxiety! Smoking not only messes your internal structure but also distorts your physical appearance drastically, and I'm sure none of us want that to happen.

So here are the straight facts. Therefore anyone who wants any of the following and really can't do with out them, then go ahead and choose which fags you like and start puffing away:

• **Lung cancer-** this was a very rare disease until the end of this century, when the medical profession witnessed a high rise in its occurrence, primarily in

Men and thereafter in women.

•Gastric Ulcers – If you don't know what that means, then you might as well forget reading the rest. Imagine, you don't even know a simple phrase like that. So if I were you I'd polish up on my English rather than trying to copy a dragon.

Chronic Bronchitis, Increase in heart rate& blood pressure. Apart from being les fit inwardly, your cheeks and skin often turn more blotchy and unsightly...Premature (ok, I'll tell you what this means 'early' OK?) ageing and more abundant **face wrinkles, heart disease, strokes,cancer** of the mouth, larynx, oesophagus, pancreas, cervix, uterus and bladder. (I haven't just made these up you know. These are thoroughly researched and proven facts)

Diminished or extinguished **sense** of smell and taste, **frequent colds**

SMOKERS COUGH- Imagine that! They have so much honour, I mean they are so unique that we have a cough named after them, huh!) And I can go on and on but I'll just stop here with a few more:

Irritability, anxiety, sleep disturbances, nervousness, headaches, fatigue, and nausea.

So if you want these then go ahead and pick anyone you wish. By the way they all have 4000 chemicals including 1200 known poisons.

Smokers: "Hey, hey you nearly killed us, now does this mean we all got these types of cancers. What were they? Pharynx, larynx, I don't know."

Sir: "Well yes if you don't stop soon enough you'll have them. But as soon as you stop your lungs begin clearing up all the toxins, it is a long process but can be done."

Smokers: Well look mate if I'm smoking 35 fags a day, I'm not saying I am but just say, right, then how in the world do I stop?

Sir: Drive a car fast and brake quickly, or if you're

not at the age where you can drive, take a train and pull the emergency communication cord.

Smokers: What!! Sir my question was about smoking, you know, with a capital S.

Sir: I know very well what your question was about. What I'm trying to do is explain that when you or someone else is driving at speed and then suddenly hits the brakes, does the car jolt to a halt? (Hey, that rhymes)

Smokers: Of course not! (Huh! What's he getting at?)

Sir: Similarly, you can't just stop smoking instantly. You'll have to do it gradually. Ill give you a living example of my very own grandpa, now aged over 70, smoked from when he was a youth. One day Allah ta'ala gave me the opportunity and I spoke to him about how one puff takes away a second of ones life away. I went on to explain that since he smoked 35 fags a day so he should cut down to 34 then 33 and so on... You won't believe it, my grandpa (regarding whom you could have said he'll never stop puffing) Alhamdulillah within a month, came to me and said, "I done it me duck! And I tell ya, I don't miss them old things."

Subhanallah! Look, if a seventy year old man can do it, then why can't you? I'm sure you're not that old physically, ok maybe mentally. Just try it and see how your life will change. You'll become a much calmer and cooler person like my granddad! Innit granddad?

Granddad: That's right me old chuck, absolutely right!

Sir: Ta, grand pa.

Smokers: ok, I'll give it a try

Sir: Don't forget to say the magic word

Smokers: Insha'allah

Sir: Excellent! Finally remember nothing can happen without His will, so effort and du'a will insha'allah get you there.

Chapter 4

Drugs & Alcohol

Allah subhanahu wata'ala has stated clearly in the Qur'an:

O you who believe! 'Khamr', gambling, idols and divining arrows are solely 'Rijs' from the handiwork of the devil. Leave it aside in order that you may be successful (Surah5 Ayah90)

OK! Two down! Don't know how many left, not much! (Hope so...)

Drugs...hmmm, sounds like a very mature 'big' & 'Manly' name don't it with a capital 'D'?

But is it really a man's business or a nut case's business? Let's see! Reason for consumption: Tasting? Feeling low?

Overcome   with problems, need some time to forget?

Been dumped by a loved one?   Or...Just feeling bored, got nothing to do?

These are the usual reasons (I said usual, if you wanna take some because you're hungry then I am sorry mate, you've lost your senses and hope you find it pretty soon) people take drugs. Because this is where people think they find?

Yes the big word, a 'BUZZ' and go around with red shot eyes, imagining themselves to be floating Aaahh... floating in the clouds... then...

WHAM!! They're back. Back to ground zero and suddenly all their problems come toppling back, only if I could get, that floating feeling back, only. No! And 'my man' goes and takes another jab or sniff then another and bang!

He has become an addict a serious addict who will not only steal to get the Buzz but also kill.First, we take a look at our guide book: has it mentioned anything about this thing that can make you forget and that can conceal our problems?

Surah Maidah (Ayah No: 90), mentioned at the beginning of this chapter puts forward the word 'KHAMR'

'Khamr' boys & girls (yes, may sound patronising and childish but just to remind you, adults don't do silly things. They tend to think before acting, you know what I mean!)

Khamr is an arabic word which means to cloud and cover. Sayyidina Umar Radhiyallahu Anhu has said 'Khamr is everything that clouds the brain' (Bukhari) So Allah Ta'ala is informing us that Kamr is rijs which means filth is messing us up internally and clouding our minds. Subhanallah in this one word Allah ta'ala has mentioned all the effects drugs and alcohol can have on a person.How consise and wonderful is His Qur'an. That book which we have left in the bookshelves only to gather dust. Only if we were to open this magnificent treasure and take effect. May Allah enable us. Ameen.

Furthermore Allah ta'ala states:
'From the works of the devil.'
Dear brothers and sisters this is the devil, the enemy of all... You are following him. (I won't say

'we' because you know I don't want to include everyone who don't wanna take drugs but are reading this chapter)

Finally, Allah ta'ala states:
"So that you may become successful, so that you may pass." If we stay away from drink and drugs, then we shall be eligible for the rewards that Allah has kept in store for us which, insha'allah, shall be discussed in great detail in the last part. Ok, that was all from the guide book Al Qur'an, let's now come and see what the prophet Sallallahu Alayhi Wasallam has said:

Sayyidina Jabir Radhiyallahu Anhu reports that the prophet Sallallahu Alayhi Wassalam said; "verily Allah ta'ala has taken it on Him that whosoever drinks intoxicants will be made to drink from 'Teenatal Khibaal'. The companions (may Allah ta'ala be pleased with them) enquired, "What is Teenatal Khibaal? The Prophet Sallallahu Alayhi Wassalam replied- "the sweat of the residents of Jahannam." (hell). (Reported by Muslim)

You think you can take that? Not me anyway! And I'm sure if you've got the slightest taste you'd never opt for such a disgusting, revolting drink! May Allah ta'ala protect us!

We have already proved that 'Khamr' and 'Muskir' Intoxicants are all in the same category and include all types of drugs, alcohol etc…
If the Intoxicator is going to be made to drink the sweat juice then obviously he will be in the same place as them, but just to make it crystal clear that boy!

If we're gonna sniff and inject, then we're heading directly away from Jannah:

Sayyidina Ibn Umar may Allah ta'ala be pleased with him said that the prophet Sallallahu Alayhi Wasallam

said, "Allah has forbidden Jannah for three types of people:
1)Consumer of Intoxicants ... (reported by Ahmed)

Just that one extract from one Hadith should be enough for a true believer to put into practice but just for emphasis, we'll quote one more Hadith:

Ibn Abbas (may Allah ta'ala be pleased with him) reports that the prophet Muhammad sallallahu alayhi wasallam said: "A person that takes intoxicants, if he dies, then he shall meet Allah like an Idol Worshipper!" (Reported by Ahmed)

Allah Akbar! Idol Worship is the greatest sin, to bow down before someone / something other then Allah ta'ala!I think that's made things extra clear and these warnings should be enough for any Muslim or Muslimah, but if you still wanna look like a person who's just come out the grave then you know, go ahead......

Remember He is ever ready, don't wait till tomorrow, do it today! Don't listen to that devil whispering to you, he only needs some company because he is doomed to hell, so to him the more the merrier.

Now the physical harms .Well the most famous ones umm.... Done with 'speed ', makes you 'crack', any other? Oh yes, don't forget ecstasy. Most drugs have professional names that don't sound fun, but people change them. e.g.

<u>LSD</u>: -Na, too hard to say, so they made 'trips', 'acid', 'tabs', and 'microdots!'
Description- Generally produced on paper squares, sometimes with a picture on them.
How is it taken - Sucked and swallowed.
Risks - From the name 'trip', once a trip has started, can't be stopped. Sometimes people feel hot, sick or dizzy makes one feel panicky and afraid. Can become mentally ill. Still sounds fun?

SPEED: Maybe you think you're too slow in life and need an artificial boost? Well let's see how fast you can become.

Technical name- amphetamines

Fun / slang names- Speed, uppers, whizz (now that sounds really interesting!) amph, sulphate (hey! I thought that was chemistry?)

Description - Dirty white or orangey yellow powder or tablets.

Reason for consumption - Makes people feel they have more energy, want to talk a lot and be raring.

Risks – the user can become aggressive, tense and scared. Bad moods and tiredness tend to result after the drug has worn off (I mean what's the point you only get energy for a few hours, and then you're in a worse state than when you started!) If taken in excess can kill by causing strain on the heart! (Huh! just for some energy you're killing yourself. I'd call this Drug "CRAZY", as another slang name)

CANNABIS sounds like a "cannibal!" (Man-eating

creature) may be it is, cause it does eat you up.

Slang names- Grass, blow, weed, spliff, ganja, dope (you will be one if you try this!) and hash

Description-Cannabis resin usually looks like small brown lumps. The leaves, stalks and seeds of the cannabis plant look like greeny brown tobacco.

Reason for taking - People think it makes them feel more relaxed and more friendly, giggly and talkative.

Risks - This drug is taken lightly by youngsters today, they falsely believe that it doesn't present them any harm.

So I ask you take a little poison it wont kill you immediately. It'll just rip your intestines out that's all! Gonna take it? Similarly, for a believer something which is haram is haram. That's it, no ifs or buts! If to take something is to remain in the disobedience of Allah ta'ala, then how can I even go near such a thing? What face will I show if I do, on the Day of Judgement?So I was saying, people underestimate this particular drug, maybe because they are a bit "dopey". But the risks are clear (you know what? I don't think I should write "risks", "results" is a better word)

Results of taking cannabis – Without being aware of it, users usually become Panicky, worried and confused, (All the qualities of a dope!), blood shot eye, dry mouth, hungry (right, this sounds like a cannibal!) causes bronchitis, lung cancer.

'O' how many left? Don't worry, just a few more and then we have some real life incidents for all of us to earn lessons from.

ECSTASY – A tablet of different colours and shapes (sounds pretty innocent!)

Slang names- E, Mitsubishis, Rolexes (that's car and watches right?)

Reasons for consumption - makes you think everyone is your friend. Huh! Can't make any friends, so try thinking everyone's your friend.

Results- It makes you frightened and dizzy once the

drug has worn off, people can feel very tired but find it very difficult to sleep. Over heating of the body may occur which can result in death! And, Depression.(You know most drugs have this effect, and the funny thing is that the drugs are usually taken to so-call 'improve problems' but it gives you the opposite effect.)

HEROIN

Slang names- H, Smack (you will get one if you don't stop, from someone) Horse, Junk (that explains it in a nutshell) Brown.

Description- off-white, browny powder, usually wrapped in small packets of paper

Reasons for consumption – Slows people down (No comments!)Drowsy, makes one feel away from the real world.

Results after consumption – addictive, death from overdose and risk of infections such as hepatitis and A.I.D.S.

COCAINE

Slang names- Coke, Snow, Charlie, C. (Man, this drug has some funny names!)

Description- White powder

Reasons for consumption- it makes people feel more energetic and confident.

Results after consumption- it can make one feel uptight, panicky, sick, sleepless, tired and depressed. Sorry mate, but just 'don't see the point and I'm sure you agree. You're taking it to become a little more energetic but you end up with all the above, plus the anger of Allah ta'ala.

That's it folks, enough facts, now lets look and study a few cases of how drugs has affected people, ready?

Before we go on, we should make it clear that the few verses and Ahadith that were mentioned with drugs in mind, also apply to alcohol.

Chapter
5

Case Studies

Case study No 1.

Name: Chris   Age: 14

"It all started about a year ago. I used to meet my mates down at the park. One day someone turned up with a refill can – it was lighter gas I think. I said 'no' but then the others all had a go and it looked like fun. It felt great, like I had no worries. After that I went down to the park a lot. We'd mess around sniffing lighter refills or glue ... anything we could get our hands on really. It was a real laugh. Then my parents started asking me questions.

They tried to stop me going out with my friends - I had to start lying to dodge them. I just started to feel so tired all the time. Eventually the headmaster asked to see me because I'd fallen asleep in class. But, I didn't care. I felt good when I was down at the park, when I was at school or at home I felt bored and sort of shut off.

Then one day, we all had a sniff of a can and one of my friends said he felt really dizzy. He fell over and just lay on the ground all curled up. None of us were laughing anymore. I was frightened...

I didn't know what to do. I ran off and got this man to

Help. He turned my friend on his side in case he was sick he said – to stop

him choking on his own vomit, he told me to cover him with my coat to keep him warm. The man wanted to get an ambulance - but my friend said he was feeling better and just didn't want his parents to find out what he'd been doing. The man told us we were really lucky – he said you can die from sniffing. Sniffing from cans- J'm finished with all that.

So here was a living example of a boy age 14. And it was a very small kind of drug. Sniffing glue and these were the results. May Allah ta'ala protect us. So many lessons to be learnt, particularly about friendship - bad friendship leads to bad experience. .Let's now look at a case study centring on another drug which has recently been classed as "Grade C", and teens are thinking its okay.

Case study No 2
CANNABIS KILLED MY BEAUTIFUL DAUGHTER

Joanna jumped to her death from a motorway bridge near her home three months ago after a ten year battle with mental illness.

Mr Barter (her father) spoke out to oppose the Governments decision to relax the law on cannabis and to warn other young people of its dangers. Joanna began smoking cannabis as a student several years ago before she showed any signs of mental health problems. As she became dependent on the drug, the mental health problems increased, she used to say,"I need the drug to make me feel more relaxed and confident."

Dr. Peter Maguire of the BMA's science committee said, "I have colleagues who are psychiatrists and they quite often say that we've seen many people with psychosis and depression after using Cannabis.

The BMA is extremely concerned that the public might think that reclassification equals safe. It does not ".

One more and that should be more than enough. Ok, we've done the so called light ones and seen life experiences; let's go to something more faster humm...SPEED!

Case study No 3
"MY LIFES A MESS"

Name: Sarah Age: 16.

"I used to think I'd never take drugs. I was happy enough. What did I need drugs for? If only things had stayed that way ....The first time I took speed I just wanted to try it once – to see what it was like .We were going to this party, and my friends said that we'd have a better night if we were off our heads. I can't remember much about the party now I felt so tired afterwards – really done in.

I started going out with these friends quite a bit – they knew where all the good parties were, we'd meet up on a Saturday night and take some 'whizz' to see us through. We were having a brilliant time. My other friends at school seemed really immature and boring.

I could never be bothered to do any homework when I got home I felt so tired. When I failed my end of year exams I had this massive row with my dad. I hated being at school and I hated being at home. I started stealing from my mum's purse to pay for the drugs and the nights out. I knew I was letting her down.

There was this big night out planned. I wanted to try some E – but I was broke. Me and a mate went into town and nicked some stuff from one department store. I was really scared we thought we'd got away with it, but then the store detective came up to me – it was the worst moment of my whole life.

The police told my parents – and now my dad won't speak to me . My friends at school have found out and they keep away from me. I never imagined this would all happen I just wish everything was back to normal ...

But alas, things can't come back to normal just like that. Dear brothers and sisters, let us take heed from these people's experiences and let us understand the reality.

In the words of a South African Scholar, "It's just quick pleasure." How true!

All the case studies we went through had fun in the beginning but then BANG!! The situations they found themselves in were unpleasant, even scary. It's really to do with how one thinks of the consequences. You know, if someone was told that if you walk into the next room you're gonna get 50 bucks but inside that room a serial killer awaits, surly no intelligent person's gonna sacrifice his neck for some bucks which he's not even gonna get to spend. Remember say "No!" once and for all to these people who offer you "poison." let it ring in their ears, let it hurt them and let them call you "immature" or "boring". But know very well that you're not immature; I can tell you that, because 'immature' according to the Oxford Collins Dictionary is. "A person not fully developed, lacking wisdom or stability." Now tell me, are you immature or is it the guy who does not know the consequences of his actions??

That shall be sufficient for this chapter, inshallah. But before we move on, just one more piece of advice to some people who themselves don't take drugs but instead deal and sell them! (It is a known fact that 99% of drug dealers don't take drugs themselves) So you guys wanna mess up other people's lives, huh? And you'll feel very happy in your conscience when spending that UNLAWFUL (haram) money?

For Allah's sake think! How can you mess innocent people's lives up for a few bucks? Please! If you know what's gonna happen to the guy then why? I mean, are you that bad that you can't get yourself a decent paying job. Well there are many "job centres" around; I suggest you pay a visit pretty soon. So, don't you ever think that the boy or girl to whom you're giving the stuff to is gonna become an addict, start to steal, get inflicted with deadly diseases, become unhealthy, not get very far in life and wring your neck if he gets the chance after all that. .Yes, you may be laughing, but it's true if not in this world then on the Day of Judgement he's gonna grab you and tell Allah ta'ala, "He took me astray!" that's not gonna free his neck, but it will give him some satisfaction to see you punished, so do give it some serious thought, with a few knocks in the brain, I'm sure you'll get through! Hopefully!

Chapter 6

Remembering Allah

Looking back at the most common reasons why young people allowed them selves to be introduced to drugs, were feeling depressed, feeling low and having nothing to do. But, none of them seem to be able to get rid of this boredom, this depression. Whereas Allah ta'ala has given us such a drug which is 100% free from any side effects, guarantees you the 'buzz' and sets you up with peace and tranquillity.

This is ZIKR.

Yes, the remembrance of Allah ta'ala. Allah the Almighty, stated In the Qur'an hundreds of years ago, for me and you, that-

"Verily through the remembrance of Allah hearts find contentment."

Just give it a try, from today: allocate some time, where you sit down and remember your Creator for everything. I swear by Him, you most definitely will find peace, such peace and happiness that no drug can

ever bring, no money can ever buy! It's all in your hands.
Dhikr of Allah ta'ala can be of many types.

A few examples:

'Subhanallah Glory be to Allah

Other names: Tasbeeh

Reasons for recitation: Peace.

Results upon recitation: Allah remembers you,
guaranteed peace, a tree is planted in your Jannah so
big that an Arabian horse would not be able to
encompass its shade even after running for a hundred
years, protected from public enemy No 1 shaytan (the
devil)

Allah ta'ala's nearness is gained And many more.

'Lailaha illallah There is no god but Allah ta'ala.

Other names: Kalimah

Reasons for recitation: Peace, gain many rewards

Results upon recitation:Peace guaranteed, entry into

Jannah if you die in the state that the Kalimah is with you, gift of your face shining like the moon on the day of Judgement if recited 100 times daily, best dhikr, protection from shaytan, Allah ta'ala's nearness is gained. And many more.

'Sallallahu Alayhi Wasallam'   May Allah's peace and blessings be upon the prophet.
Other names: 'Salat Alan Nabi'
Reasons for recitation: Pleasing Allah. Peace etc.
Results upon recitation :One who recites once Allah Ta'ala:
Forgives 10 of his sins, sends 10 mercies to him, elevates him 10 ranks in Jannah, the more recited the more closer will be to the prophet sallallahu alayhi wasallam, Angels also send mercy, Protection from the devil and nearness of Allah ta'ala is gained.

<u>Astagfirullah</u>   I seek forgiveness from Allah.

Other names: Istigfar

Reasons for reciting: To please Allah & to Repent.

Results upon recitation: He who continues to recite Astagfirullah then Allah ta'ala will:

Make an exit for him from any hardship, ease every worry and problem, sustain him from where he had no hope,forgive his sins, protect him from the devil and Allah ta'ala's nearness is gained.

Allahu Akbar! These were just the tip of the iceberg, when it comes to the side-effects free drugs Allah ta'ala has gifted us with. Look at the reasons from reciting and the results, don't they coincide? Don't they match? Drugs of shaytan are totally opposite

Ok, that's it, take a break before you read the next chapter because you must have got exhausted by this one..

May Allah ta'ala protect us. Remember the key is-

"ED"
"Effort and Du'a"

Bet you thought that was another drugs slang name?
Never know could be some day...

Chapter
7

Du'aa

A Christian lady was once asked as to what encouraged her to become a Muslim, she said ' the relationship that I saw between the creator and the creation in Islam was second to none. It is truly a connection of a lover and his beloved.

Subhannallah it's true man. If we check all the masnoon Adiyah we have been encouraged and shown to pray by our beloved messenger Sallalaahu Alayhi Waslallam then we'll realise that a rapport is being built between us and our creator that wherever we may be we are reminded that we are never alone and he is there for us. Let's look at a few translations of some adiyah.

When we sleep at night we say oh Allah in your name do I die and live, waking up; oh Allah I thank you for giving me life after death, exiting the toilet; oh Allah thank you for relieving me from the harmful substances, before we eat; oh Allah bless this food in your name do i begin, after we eat; Oh Allah thank you for granting me food and drink and making me one of the believers. And we can carry on, but I guess you might start thinking your in madressa , but truly amazing it is that we are making du'a to Allah at all instances in our life. Let us try to understand the depth of all these adiyah next time we pray them.

So what is du'a and how should one make du'a and why is it that we sometimes feel and see our requests not being accepted?

Allah ta'ala has stated in the qur'an
"When my servants ask you concerning me. I am indeed close to them. I answer the prayer of every caller when he calls unto me." (Surah 2 Ayah 186)

So Allah ta'ala is telling us all that he answers every prayer. And, we, Allah forbid think differently. The answer is guys that we truly do not know how to ask from his limitless treasures.

This incident should explain what I mean:

Once the king Hajjaj ibn Yusuf was doing Tawaf of the Kabah in Makkah Mukarramah and he passed by a blind man who was saying 'Oh Allah give me eyes, give me eyes, give me eyes... Continuously he was saying these phrases. Hajjaj became very perturbed for each round he heard hi m like a parrot. So he got hold of him and said i have been listening to you for so long asking from Allah, but Allah still has not given you eyes. I'm fed up. If you can't see by the end of my tawaf (Tawaf is seven circuits around the cubic shaped building known as the kabah) then i shall have you killed and he deployed two soldiers to watch the blind man. Now Hajjaj was known for his tyranny and for keeping his word. If he said he'll kill someone then boy oh boy he meant it. The blind man began sweating buckets and fell to the floor and pleaded to Allah in desperation; 'Oh Allah if you do not give me my eyesight then i shall be no more. Oh Allah I beg of you. Please.. And he cried like never before.

As Hajaj completed his Tawaf he called the blind man

and to everyone's happiness he could see! Subhanallah. Hajjaj looked at him and smiled ' Fool! That is how you make dua to Allah. Show Allah you really want the thing you are asking for. Don't just speak like a parrot without paying attention to what you are saying.

What an important lesson for us all. Do we really ask Allah for our needs in desperation? Think when a child wants something from his parent how does he behave? How does he plead and cry?

Sadly sometimes we just ask Allah when we are in trouble or need something. A Muslim must always communicate with Allah. In happy moments praise and thank him and in difficult moments seek and plead from him. There was once a person who was seen in a particular masjid crying to Allah, having grown a beard and in the first line. For a few weeks no one saw him then the imam met himin the shops; beard gone ear phones on and Islamic dress vanished. Upon inquiry he said oh I needed Allah bec. my wife had done a runner.

But she's back now so its ok!

Imagine that huh!

Here are a few etiquettes of making Du'a

Praise Alla h first.

Send Salutaions Upon the best of Mankind Muhammad Sallallahu Alayhi wasallam.

Begin your du'a by asking Allah of your own needs and then move on to your family & friends (if you can squeeze me and my family and teachers in... Thanks mate.) Don't forget to Ask Allah for the needs of the hereafter.

Send salutations upon Rasulullah Sallallahu Alayhi Wasallam

End with the praises of Allah ta'ala.

One should try to keep both hands in line with the chest, a slight gap in between and after dua'a pass your hands over your face. Some people think we should not do this passing hands over our face but you should ok. Here's the proof from the Hadith:

Ibn Abbas Radhiyallahu Anhu narrates that the

Messenger Sallallahu Alayhi Wasallam said: '... When you complete your dua'a then pass your hands over your face.'
(Narrated by ibn Majah which is one of six authentic books of Hadith.)

One last important thing we must remember is that if the food we eat is haram then our du'as shall not be accepted, so please check before consuming anything.

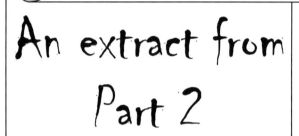

An extract from
Part 2

OUT NOW!

**WHEN YOU CAME INTO THE WORLD, SHE HELD YOU IN HER ARMS
YOU THANKED HER BY WAILING LIKE A BANSHEE...**

**WHEN YOU WERE 1 YEARS OLD, SHE FED YOU AND BATHED YOU
YOU THANKED HER BY CRYING ALL NIGHT...**

**WHEN YOU WERE 2 YEARS OLD, SHE TAUGHT YOU TO WALK
YOU THANKED HER BY RUNNING AWAY WHEN SHE CALLED...**

"My old man just can't keep it shut!"

"Nag! Nag! Nag! That's all he does all day!"

"Come on man, what do they know??? What faintest idea do they have of what's it like living in the modern ages? Huh! Just think everyone's like them"

Ever heard those words from your own mouth? Or maybe from others? Sadly, these are the usual sentences people use to describe their parents! Yes, dear brothers and sisters, it may seem that your parents are always nagging at you for whatever reason, but you have got to get this right:

if it weren't for our parents then we would never have existed, and if they hadn't looked after us then we would never have got to the age to read this.

Who was the one who stayed awake all night worrying and caring for you? Who was it that sweated all day so you could have the best clothes?

Who was the one that forgave you a thousand and one times...?

It's true guys, we've really gotta think when we're at boiling points with our parents, that at the end of the day these people whom I'm about to explode upon are the actual cause of my existence in this world. What must they be going through at that very moment in time? When their once beautiful bouncing baby boy or girl starts threatening to bounce them?

**WHEN YOU WERE 3 YEARS OLD, SHE MADE ALL YOUR MEALS WITH LOVE
YOU THANKED HER BY TOSSING YOUR PLATE ON THE FLOOR...**

**WHEN YOU WERE 4 YEARS OLD, SHE GAVE YOU SOME CRAYONS
YOU THANKED HERE BY COLOURING THE DINING ROOM TABLE...**

**WHEN YOU WERE 5 YEARS OLD, SHE DRESSED YOU FOR THE HOLIDAYS
YOU THANKED HER BY PLOPPING INTO THE NEAREST PILE OF MUD...**

**WHEN YOU WERE 6 YEARS OLD, SHE WALKED YOU TO SCHOOL
YOU THANKED HER BY SCREAMING, "I'M NOT GOING!"**

Let's go a little into the future and catapult ourselves into their position:

Here we are, fifty years from today chilling at home oops sorry we won't be chilling at that age will we? Let's say breathing at home... having worked our guts out for our children, who've grown up now and seem to be fairly independent. Now, here I am sitting at home all day waiting for my ickle cuddly child to come and then I can listen to his day's activities and adventures...

Suddenly he/she comes barging in...

Flings the bag on the floor...

Storms upstairs...

And ' bang!' goes the bedroom door.

Let me see what's wrong... I climb the stairs gently...

To be continued...

An extract from
Part 3

Coming

soon . . .

End of school day

Girl 1: see ya.
Boy: Yeah you too.
Girl1: Take care, Gonna miss you. Cum on Msn ok! We'll
chat.
Boy: k.

Half an hour later...

www.msn.co.uk
Girl 1 :Hi you ok?
Boy: Yeah you? What you doing?
Girl 1: Nothing much.
Boy: I luv u
Girl 1: Me2

Suddenly an add pops up wanting to join
Allow?
Boy: Yes.
Hi ASL?
Boy: 16 M UK. You?
Girl 2: 16 F USA.

Previous screen pops up.

Girl 1: hey where do you go to?
Boy: O sos I'm busy ma old man s calling me catch you
later.

Girl 1: Oah!
Boy: Sos man gotta go.
Girl1: Okay. Xxx

Back on new screen.

Girl 2: You free?
Boy: Yeah you?
Girl2: Yep!
Boy: Got web cam?
Girl2: Yes sir.
Boy: Wanna see you. send ur pic.
Picture appears.
Boy: Wow. You look a beauty. Xxx
Girl 2: So do you wanna be friends?
Boy: more than friends!

To be continued......

Also by An Nasihah
Publications specially for
girls...

THE HIJAB

Umme Muhammad

Coming soon...

The Hijab shall inshallah cover all aspects relating to young girls, issues such as the concept of Hijab, Periods etc, will be discussed in detail. An extract from one article in the book :

'What the eye don't see the heart don't desire!'

Check this article out!

"I have a story to tell so sit back with ease and take heed of what I am about to say. I was once young, full of the vigour of youth, blessed with good looks and a personality to match. Everyday was a new adventure for me. I took no heed form my parents... The world was my oyster. I had no worries. Life was for living! I was carefree. Males desired me, females envied me. Life was wonderful. That was a few years ago.. Little did I know how my life would change..."

To be continued...

farewell... wassalam

Please send your comments, suggestions and questions regarding any teen issues you have or about any of our publications to

theworldof_teens@yahoo.com

Or if you don't wanna get caught in the web then write to:

An Nasihah

PO BOX 7737

LEICESTER

LE5 5XU

UK.

BIBLIOGRAPHY

The meaning of the Glorious Qur'an.
Abdullah Yusuf Ali.
Amana Publications

Tambihul Ghafilin.
Abu Layth Samarqandi.
Darul Kutub Al Arabiya Beirut.

Mishkaat ul Masaabeeh
Abu Muhammad Husayn ibn Masud Bagawi
Qadimi Kutub Khana.

Zadul Talibeen
Muhammad Ashiq Ilahi Al Barni
Prudence Publications.

Misbahul Lugat
Abu fadl Moulana Abdul Hafiz Balawi
Darul Isha'at.

Music Exposed.
Siraj Ibn Yusuf Lambat
Time Publications